Handwriting
Workout Cursive

by
Renee Cummings

Cover Design
by
Peggy Jackson

Inside Illustrations
by
Pat Biggs and
Alyson Higginbotham

Published by Instructional Fair • TS Denison
an imprint of

McGraw-Hill
Children's Publishing

About the Author

Renee Cummings, with eighteen years of classroom teaching experience in the primary grades, has developed much insight into the needs and abilities of young students. She is an experienced author, having written numerous books for the Instructional Fair brand. Renee holds a bachelor's degree in elementary education from Oregon State University.

McGraw-Hill Children's Publishing is proud to have an author with Renee's talent writing creative and exciting activities for young students. She resides in Hood River, Oregon, with her husband, who currently presides as the town's mayor.

Credits

Author: Renee Cummings
Cover Design: Peggy Jackson
Inside Illustrations: Pat Biggs and
                          Alyson Higginbotham
Project Director/Editor: Sharon Kirkwood
Editors: Sara Bierling, Mary Hassinger,
              Kathryn Wheeler
Page Design: Sandra Harris

McGraw-Hill
Children's Publishing

A Division of The McGraw-Hill Companies

Published by Instructional Fair • TS Denison
An imprint of McGraw-Hill Children's Publishing
Copyright © 2000 McGraw-Hill Children's Publishing

Send all inquiries to:
McGraw-Hill Children's Publishing
3195 Wilson Drive NW
Grand Rapids, Michigan 49544

Handwriting Workout—Cursive
ISBN: 1-56822-907-0

Table of Contents

Introduction

Handwriting is not as easy as it seems! Small muscle control, hand/eye coordination, memory, and letter–sound association have very important roles in handwriting. The activities in this book have been designed to provide practice and help to further develop these important skills.

The first section of *Handwriting Workout* provides activities to practice basic movements needed for cursive writing. Pencil control and hand/eye coordination are practiced by drawing lines through a multi-solution maze and tracing over dotted lines to complete a picture.

Following the prewriting activities are pages of individual lowercase letters. They are divided into categories according to the movement needed for the formation of the letter. This division helps students focus on a specific movement pattern, which they can then associate with the letter. There are two pages for each letter. The first provides practice of the letter plus words containing the letter in different positions in the words: initial, medial, and final. The second page provides practice of the letter plus phrases with words that contain the specific letter.

Capital letters are addressed in the third section of the book. As with lowercase letters, the capitals are also grouped in categories according to similar movement, with two pages for each letter. The first provides practice of the capital letter and words beginning with the capital letter. The second page provides practice of sentences beginning with the specific capital letter. Words containing its lowercase partner are used to create the remainder of each sentence.

The last section of the book provides practice using both lowercase and capital letters. Two of these pages address writing numbers and number words from one to twenty. Because daily school and activity schedules are becoming more and more important, there are pages devoted to writing the days of the week and the months of the year. The remaining pages provide activities that require the student to view words written in manuscript and then to write them in cursive.

Encouragement is one of the best motivators for students. Have students strive for neatness and legibility. *Handwriting Workout* provides a good basic model for handwriting practice. Although some schools may use a different program, the basic movements are standard to all programs, and slight variations should not be a problem.

Name

Swooping Feathers

Trace the dotted lines. Then continue the pattern.

Trace the dotted lines. Then complete the picture.

© Instructional Fair • TS Denison

Sharp, Curvy Teeth

Trace the dotted lines. Then continue the pattern.

Name _____

Trace the dotted lines. Then complete the picture.

Name _____

In Control

Trace the dotted lines. Then continue the pattern.

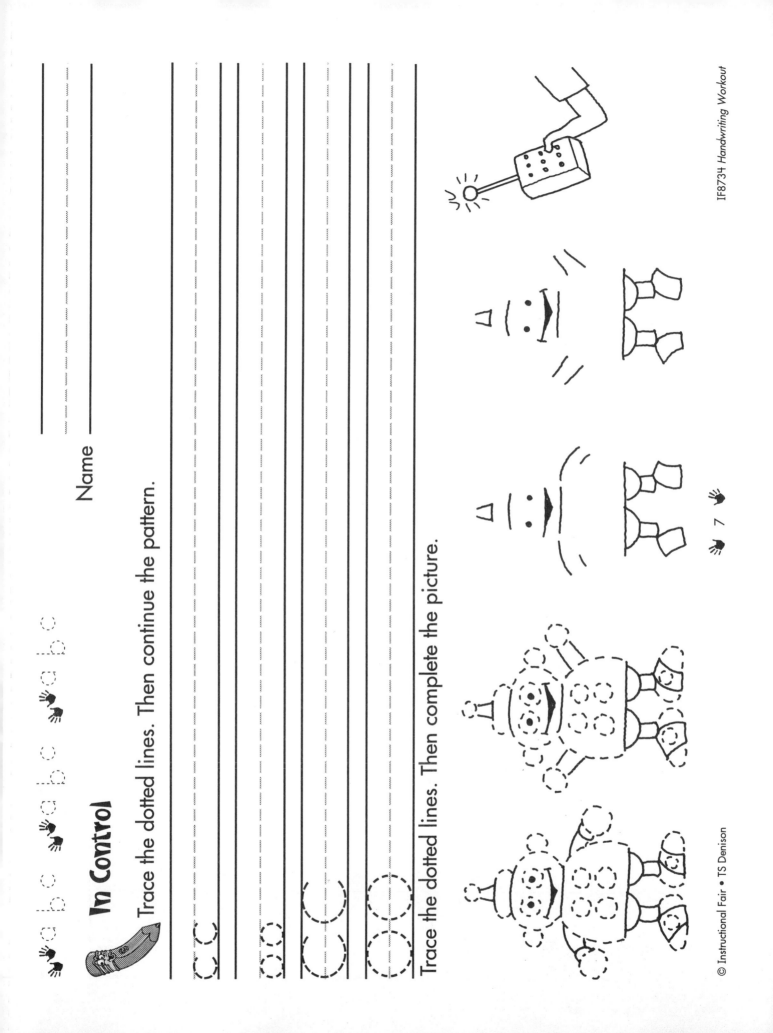

Trace the dotted lines. Then complete the picture.

7

Moving Down the Court

Name _____

Trace the dotted lines. Then continue the pattern.

Trace the dotted lines. Then complete the picture.

A Looping Connection

Trace the dotted lines. Then continue the pattern.

Trace the dotted lines. Then complete the picture.

© Instructional Fair • TS Denison

IF8734 *Handwriting Workout*

Curly and Crunchy

Name _____

Trace the dotted lines. Then continue the pattern.

Trace the dotted lines. Then complete the picture.

Super Curly Fries

A Slanting Baleen

Trace the dotted lines. Then continue the pattern.

Trace the dotted lines. Then complete the picture.

Name _____

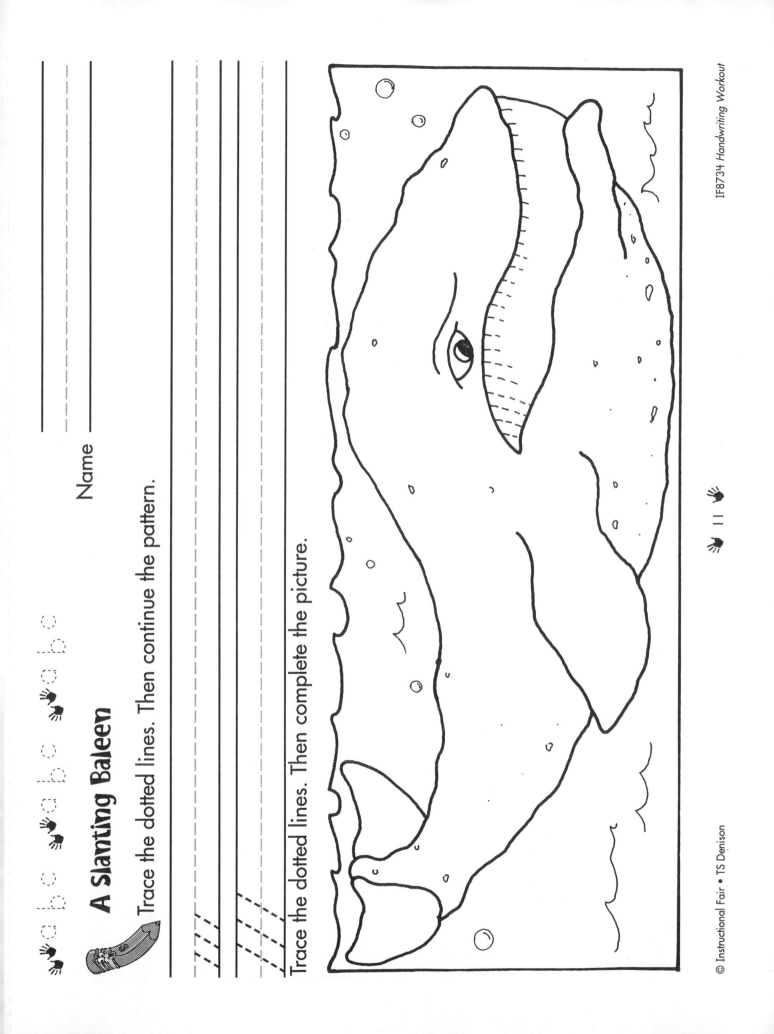

IF8734 Handwriting Workout

Name _____

Downny Wings

Trace the dotted lines. Then continue the pattern.

Trace the dotted lines. Then complete the picture.

IF8734 Handwriting Workout

Name _____

Gently Curving Spine

Trace the dotted lines. Then continue the pattern.

Trace the dotted lines. Then complete the picture.

IF8734 Handwriting Workout

Alligator's Swampy Path

Draw a line through the maze to show the different ways the alligator can go to reach the water.

Name _____

Name _____

Lots of Space

Trace the dotted lines to complete the picture.

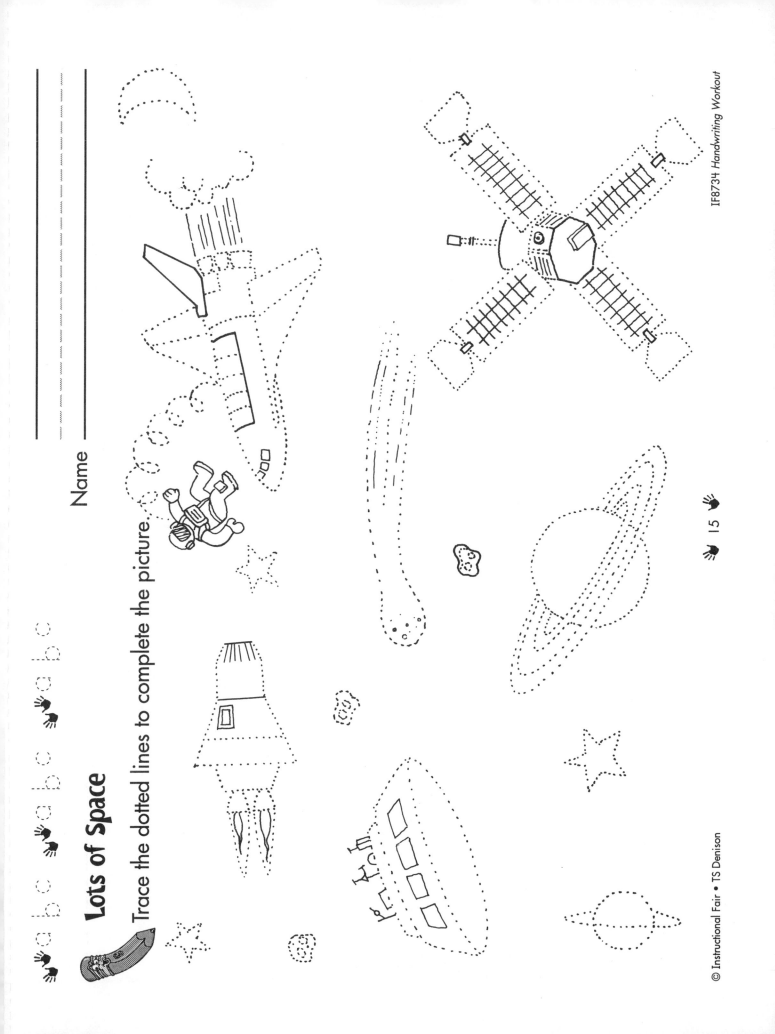

IF8734 Handwriting Workout

Write the letter and words.

i

instruments

inspection

magnificent

spaghetti

invitation

Name _____

Write the letter and phrases.

i

inactive iguana

whirling rapids

qualified musician

irrigation sprinkler

spicy chili

17

t

Write the letter and words.

t t t t

triceratops

meteorite

ultralight

partners

respected

Name

t

Write the letter and phrases.

t t

theater ticket

postage stamp

street traffic

nature trail

knotted string

IF8734 Handwriting Workout

Name _____

u o b c o o b c o o b c o

Write the letter and words.

u

u u u u u u

unplug

plateau

museum

future

uranium

u u u u u u u u u u

u

Write the letter and phrases.

u u u

unusual urns

restaurant menu

parachute jumper

lunar launch

southern route

21

Name _____

w w w w w w w

w

Ww Ww Ww

whistles

snowplow

write

whirlwind

unknown

Name _____

Write the letter and phrases.

w

warm waffles

new owner

twisted turns

lawn mower

brawny crew

Write the letter and words.

N

refrigerator

armchair

geography

errands

proprietor

24

Name _____

Write the letter and phrases.

R r

roaming reindeer

sports arena

gritty sandpaper

chirping crickets

raspberry tart

25

Write the letter and words.

S

S S S S

sweatshirts

fossils

scientist

biscuits

essay

Name

ll ll ll ll ll

Write the letter and phrases.

Ll

space shuttle

delicious desserts

science lesson

sunflower seeds

scenic hillside

c

Write the letter and words.

c

c c c

cockatoo

classic

bicycle

chocolate

microscope

Name

c c c c c c c c c

c

Write the letter and phrases.

c c

computer chip

grocery sack

music recital

secret lock

dramatic actor

IF8734 Handwriting Workout

a b c a b c a b c
a b c a b c

Write the letter and words.

o o o

orbiting

locomotive

doorknob

motto

mongoose

Name _____

Write the letter and phrases.

o

ably volcans

school programs

tropical rainforest

bountiful crops

howling hounds

Write the letter and words.

a

a a a a

armadillo

applesauce

papaya

salamander

tarantula

Name

Write the letter and phrases.

a a

athletic teams

pasta salad

panda bear

haul away

lazy day

Name _____

Write the letter and words.

d

d d

dinosaurs

handstand

addition

legend

dodged

Name _____

d

Write the letter and phrases.

d d

dining board

weed the garden

gold medallions

good advice

road detour

n

Write the letter and words.

n

n n n n

nutrition

tunnel

innkeeper

pronoun

fountain

Name _____

m n o p q r s t u v w x y z

m

Write the letter and phrases.

m m m

nutty nougat

glowing lantern

skinny pencils

talent contest

narrow lanes

Write the letter and words.

m

m

m m m

manatee

important

homonym

tumbling

minimum

Name _____

m m m m m m m m m m m m m

m

Write the letter and phrases.

m mm

massive mastodon

farm machinery

mushy macaroni

common stamp

creamy caramels

39

Name _____

Write the letter and words.

v

volleyball

discovery

resolve

interview

marriage

Write the letter and phrases.

𝓏

various volumes

visiting relatives

seven novels

microwave oven

movie review

Write the letter and words.

x

xylophones

relax

lynx

texture

expedition

42

Name _____

Write the letter and phrases.

x x x x x

xx saxophones

boxing exhibition

exact tan

exciting textbooks

sixty examples

Name _____

Write the letter and words.

e

e e e

engineer

refer

feature

interested

league

a b c a b c a b c

Name

ℓ

Write letter and phrases.

ℓℓ ℓ

exercise equipment

telephone line

model airplane

dress rehearsal

new experience

ℓ

ololololol

Write the letter and words.

ℓ ℓ ℓ

leopards

million

brilliant

local

infield

Name

Write the letters and phrases.

$\mathscr{L}$ l

lively lobsters

blueberry bagel

library shelf

vanilla float

helicopter flight

© Instructional Fair • TS Denison

Write the letter and words.

Ll

Ll Ll Ll

frosted

climb

habitat

petite

library

Name _____

Write the letter and phrases.

f

fk

baked beans

bread crumbs

library book

trifling balloon

beef and cabbage

49

© Instructional Fair • TS Denison

IF8734 *Handwriting Workout*

H

Write the letter and words.

H H H H H H

h h h

horseshoes

highway

autograph

whirlpool

Name _____

h · h · h · h · h · h

h

Write the letter and phrases.

h h

hefty hippos

chrome finish

another choice

with a sigh

shallow harbor

51

k k k k k c k c k c

Kk

Write the letter and words.

Kk Kk

basketball

knuckles

ticket

bookkeeping

haystack

52

Name _____

k k k k k k k k k

k

Write the letter and phrases.

k k

kindly koalas

wicker basket

thick milkshake

striking fireworks

squawking hawk

53

Write the letter and words.

f ff

firefighter

cliff

frankfurter

mischief

drifting

Name _____

ffffffff

Write the letter and phrases.

F f

film festival

different flavors

brief definition

crafty fox

stiff feathers

Name _____

Write the letter and words.

J j

𝒥

J J

jackhammer

journalist

projector

adjective

majestic

56

Name _____

Write the letter and phrases.

$\mathcal{J}$

jaunty jonquils

major adjustment

jubilant judge

majestic jewels

enjoyable journey

Name _____

Write the letter and words.

p

$\mathcal{p}$ $\mathcal{p}$ $\mathcal{p}$

pineapple

newspaper

crisp

wrapped

promptly

58

Name _____

p p p p p p p p p p

p

Write the letter and phrases.

P p

pepperoni pizza

sparkling sapphire

laptop computer

wrapping paper

pecan pie

y

Write the letter and words.

y y y

y y y

yummy

symphony

mystery

boysenberry

60

Name _____

Write the letter and the phrases.

Y y

yonder yacht

royal family

loyal buddy

healthy gymnast

young python

Name _____

Write the letter and words.

z

zucchini

z z z z

why

watched

hazy

bulldozer

Name _____

Z z z z z z

Write the letter and phrases.

Zz Zz

zigzagging zebra

dazzling zircons

grazing gazelle

dozen prizes

amazing bazaar

IF8734 Handwriting Workout

Name _____

abc abc abc

Write the letter and words.

g

g g g g g

glacier

gadgets

suggestion

tugging

programming

64

Name

g

Write the letter and phrases.

Gg

gaggle of geese

foreign language

weighty luggage

large margins

great privilege

65

Q q

Write the letter and words.

Q q Q q

quadruplets

aquarium

sequence

earthquake

requirement

Name _____

Name _____

$$\begin{array}{r} 4 \\ \times 3 \\ \hline 12 \end{array} \qquad \begin{array}{r} 7 \\ \times 4 \\ \hline \end{array} \qquad \begin{array}{r} 8 \\ \times 6 \\ \hline \end{array}$$

Write the letter and phrases.

Qq

quick quiz

frequently requested

aquatic requirements

equal quadrangles

quietly squeaks

© Instructional Fair • TS Denison

Name _____

Cc

Write the letter and words.

C

Cc Cc Cc

Cc Cc Cc

Corpus Christi

Chenoweth

Clarence

Carolyn

68

Name _____

c a b c a b c a b c a b c

C

Write the sentences.

Chuck pulled the parachute ripcord.

_____

Carla punctuated the sentence correctly.

_____

Cheetahs race across the countryside.

_____

69

Name _____

Write the letter and words.

O O

O O

Osaka

Ottawa

Orville

Orlando

Olivia

Name _____

O O O o o o o o o o o

Write the sentences.

Orchids grow in tropical rainforests.

Otters enjoy floating on top of the water.

Otto looks for old rock formations.

abc abc abc abc

𝒜

Write the letter and words.

𝒜𝒶

𝒜𝒶𝒶𝒶

Ann Arbor

Ashland

Andrew

Alberta

72

Name _____

a b c a b c a b c

a

Write the sentences.

Alligators prowl above the swampy waters.

Athletes practice daily before a game.

An albatross eagle soars overhead.

IF8734 Handwriting Workout

E e e b e b c e b c e b c

E

Name _____

Write the letter and words.

E E

E E

Edgewood

England

Evelyn

Eugene

Name _____

Write the sentences.

Ellie planted vegetables in the garden.

Emma saved a seat for her friend.

Ed played in a soccer exhibition.

Write the letter and words.

$\mathcal{N}$

$\mathcal{N}$ $\mathcal{N}$ $\mathcal{N}$

n n n

Northampton

Newfoundland

Natasha

Nerble

Name _____

Nn

Write the sentences.

Nora listens to the noisy monkeys.

Ned opened a new business on the corner.

Nutmeg and cinnamon are wonderful spices.

77

IF8734 Handwriting Workout

m m m m m

Write the letter and words.

M M M M M M

m m m m m m

Minneapolis

Medford

Marian

Millicent

m o b o o b o o b o

M

Write the sentences.

Moose roam in the meadow.

Mike remembered his math homework.

Meg wrote a poem about animals.

Name _____

U

Write the letter and words.

U U U U U

u u u u

Umatilla

Underwood

Uruguay

Ursula

Name

U

u a b c a b c a b c

Write the sentences.

Ursula put the suitcases in the trunk.

Urs fruit a sturdy cupboard.

It usually sounds upset the emu.

IF8734 Handwriting Workout

Name _____

$\mathcal{W}$

Write the letter and words.

$\mathcal{W}\,\mathcal{W}$

$\mathcal{W}$

Walla Walla

Wenatchee

Wilfred

Wendy

Name _____

W w w w w w w w w

W

Write the sentences.

Whirling winds blow snow everywhere.

Wanda unwound the twisted twine.

Weasels swish down powdery snowflakes

𝒱

𝓋 𝒶 𝒷 𝒸 𝓋 𝒶 𝒷 𝒸

Write the letter and words.

𝒱 𝒱 𝒱

𝓋 𝓋 𝓋

Vicksburg

Veracruz

Valeria

Vincent

Name _____

Write the sentences.

Uncle avoids driving on unpaved roads.

I am investigating the cave.

Val observed a beaver in the river.

Name _____

Write the letter and words.

$\mathcal{Y}$

Yy Yy

Yakima

Yellowstone

Yvette

Yolanda

86

Name _____

abc abc abc

𝒴

Write the sentences.

Yvette plays cymbals in the symphony.

Yolanda really enjoys gymnastics.

Yves enjoys a mystery story.

Write the letter and words.

Zachary
Zane
Zave
Zampta
Zg
Zg

Name _____

GRRRR

Rr

Write the sentences.

Zoe was amazed by the grizzly bear.

Zachary bought a dozen frozen pizzas.

Zinnias and azaleas bloom near the gazebo.

Q Q Q Q Q Q Q

Write the letter and words.

Q Q Q

Q Q Q

Quincy

Quinn

Quentin

Queenie

Name

Write the sentences.

Quilts require quantities of cloth squares.

Quince frequently repairs aquatic equipment.

Quinn requested plaques for the banquet.

Name _____

Write the letter and words.

S S S

S S

S S

Sshpring

Staby

Luan

Lsabella

Name _____

Write the sentences.

I can find the light switch.

Imagine writes exciting stories.

Ida hikes a different trail each time.

IF8734 *Handwriting Workout*

Name _____

Write the letter and words.

J J J

Jacksonville

Jerome

Jennifer

Jonathan

Name _____

Write the sentences.

Justin adjusted the projector.

Ruby adjusted the old jalopy engine.

Joe yearned left for a jeep ride.

© Instructional Fair • TS Denison

Name _____

Write the letter and words.

T

Tallahassee

Turkey

Tanya

Theodore

Name _____

a b c a b c a b c

Write the sentences.

Ed stores the trunk in the attic.

Tom bought two tickets for the matinee.

Theresa is a talented artist.

Name _____

Write the letter and words.

Ff

Ff

Frankfort

Farmington

Fernando

Florence

a b c a b c a b c

Name ____________________

F

Write the sentences.

Fran ate a fruit-filled muffin.

Five fawns ran swiftly into the forest.

Fred worked the fractions by himself.

H

Write the letter and words.

H H H

H H H

Hillsboro

Hamilton

Humphrey

Helga

Name _____

abc abc abc abc

H

Write the sentences.

Huge machines load heavy freight.

Veda likes ham and cheese sandwiches.

Hippos have tough hides.

Name _____

$\mathcal{K}$

Write the letter and the words.

$\mathcal{K}$ $\mathcal{K}$ $\mathcal{K}$

$\mathcal{K}$ $\mathcal{K}$ $\mathcal{K}$

Kenya

Kentucky

Kevin

Katrina

Name _____

Write the sentences.

Kyle likes kayaking on weekends.

Karen hikes around a sparkling lake.

Kerin fed the cackling chickens.

103

X

Name _____

Write the letter and words.

X X X X

X X X

Xerxes

Xavier

Xian

Xanadu

Name

abc abc abc abc

K

Write the sentences.

Karen watched a boxing exhibition.

Kenya relaxes after exertive exercises.

Karen fixed the extension cord.

IF8734 Handwriting Workout

Write the letter and words.

Gg Gg

Gladstone
Garibaldi
Erma
Gordon

Name

Write the sentences.

Gizman is clipping the overgrown hedge.

Gus is repairing the sagging garage roof.

Glenda guided the sleigh over rough ground.

Write the letter and words.

Name _____

S S S

Sweden

Sheridan

Simon

Suzanne

Name _____

Write the sentences.

Sparkling fireworks burst in the sky.

Spirited horses race across grassy fields.

Steamboat cruises stop at historic sites.

109

Name

Write the letters and words.

$\mathcal{L}$

$\mathcal{L}$ $\mathcal{L}$

$\mathcal{l}$ $\mathcal{l}$

Latoia

Laura

Lincoln

Lois

Name _____

Write the sentences.

Laura plays the clarinet well.

Les lost his wallet at the library.

Lou lounged by the fireplace.

Write the letter and words.

D d

Dd Dd

Dd Dd

Dd Dd

Dadwood

Dayton

Douglas

Diana

Name _____

Write the sentences.

Divers found old gold medallions.

_____

I am watched thundercloud form.

_____

Drivers dodge around road hazards.

_____

P p

Write the letter and words.

P p P p

P p P p

Panama

Pollyanna

Pendleton

Phillip

Name _____

P

Write the sentences.

Pat peers through a telescope.

Pam inspected the laptop computer.

Pete tops pancakes with maple syrup.

IF8734 Handwriting Workout

Write the letter and words.

P

P P P

P P P

Paso Robles

Padding

Potosta

 Parent Ridge

Rutherford

Name

R

Write the sentences.

Rafting requires careful maneuvering.

Raccoons are curious and frisky animals.

Reindeer survive in arctic regions.

IF8734 *Handwriting Workout*

B b b b b b b b b b

$\mathcal{B}$

Write the letter and words.

$\mathcal{B}$

$\mathcal{B}\ \mathcal{B}\ \mathcal{B}\ \mathcal{B}$

$\mathcal{B}\ \mathcal{B}$

Beaumont

Butt

Barbara

Buxton

Name _____

ß

Write the sentences.

Bob observed bees building a honeycomb.

Bill steered the tugboat back to the harbor.

Beth labeled each botanical exhibit.

Pick a Number

Name _____

Write the numbers and number words.

1 one

2 two

3 three

4 four

5 five

6 six

7 seven

8 eight

9 nine

10 ten

Time for Teens

Write the numbers and number words.

Name _____

11 eleven

12 twelve

13 thirteen

14 fourteen

15 fifteen

16 sixteen

17 seventeen

18 eighteen

19 nineteen

20 twenty

IF8734 *Handwriting Workout*

Months of the Year

Write the months of the year.

January

February

March

April

May

June

Name _____

Months of the Year (cont.)

Write the months of the year.

July

August

September

October

November

December

IF8734 *Handwriting Workout*

One Day at a Time

Write the names of the days of the week.

Sunday

Monday

Tuesday

Wednesday

Thursday

Friday

Saturday

Name _____

Footprints from the Past

Name _____

Choose eight dinosaurs. Write their names in cursive on the lines.

Stegosaurus	Tyrannosaurus	Brachiosaurus
Iguanodon	Parasaurolophus	Ankylosaurus
Velociraptor	Triceratops	Pteranodon
Diplodocus	Dimetrodon	Apatosaurus

1. _____

2. _____

3. _____

4. _____

5. _____

6. _____

7. _____

8. _____

wabc wabc

At Home

Read the name of each animal. If the animal could live on a farm, write F on the line. If the animal lives in the wild, write W on the line. Then on the lines under the correct heading write the names of the animals in cursive.

_____ grizzly bear   _____ cat   _____ horse   _____ leopard
_____ dog   _____ sheep   _____ orangutan   _____ boa constrictor
_____ anteater   _____ lizard   _____ goat   _____ chicken
_____ pig   _____ tiger   _____ cow   _____ elephant

Farm

Wild

Be a Composer

Choose one word or phrase from each list (A, B, C, and D) to compose your own sentences. Write your sentences on the lines in cursive.

A	B	C	D
Beautiful	weightlifters	arched	in the gym.
Thick	sheep	grazed	in the pasture.
Husky	rainbows	exercised	the mountain peak.
Woolly	fog	surrounded	across the sky.

1. _____

2. _____

3. _____

4. _____

abc abc

Writer's Whim

Name _____

Choose one word or phrase from each list (A, B, C, and D) to compose your own sentences. Write your sentences on the lines in cursive.

A	B	C	D
Gentle	worms	march	in the ocean.
Squirmy	gerbils	swim	in the parade.
Playful	manatees	frolic	into the ground.
Trained	horses	burrow	in the cage.

1. _____

2. _____

3. _____

4. _____